ISBN: 9798739873583

Some historians refer to the 1970's or Seventies as "A United States in Flux". It was a time of great changes. For some Americans, it was a time of "self-realization" and "self-fulfillment" and for others, it was concern and care for the environment.

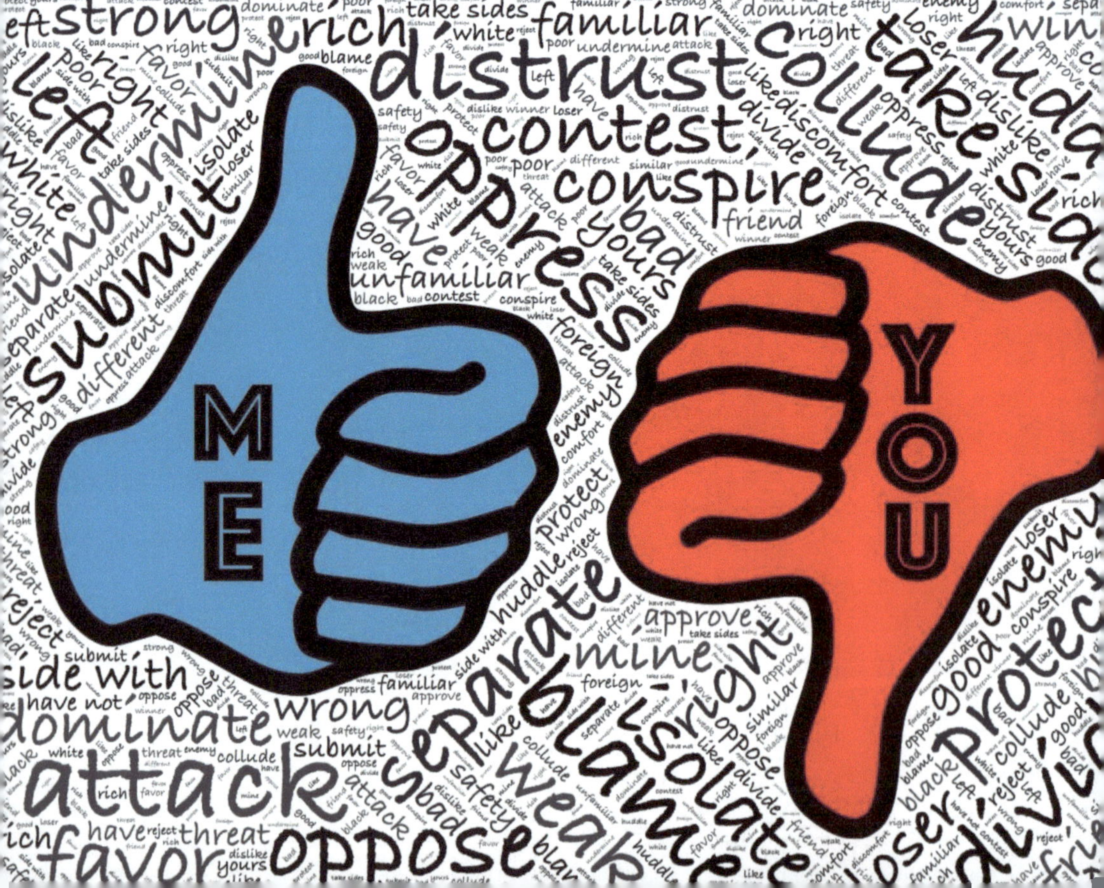

Hippies wanted to free themselves from the restrictions of American society, to find their own way of enlightenment and to discover the meaning of life.
By the early 1970's, the hippie style had been integrated into some of the American mainstream. The "V" sign of two fingers meant "Peace, Love, and Do Your Own Thing".

Alice Walker was an American novelist, short story writer, poet, black feminist, and social activist for equal rights for women.

Gloria Steinem was an American feminist, journalist and social political activist. She co-founded Ms. Magazine.

The first Earth Day celebration was held on April 22, 1970. Many Americans participated in anti-pollution demonstrations. These demonstrations included school children walking to school instead of riding the bus.

On May 4, 1970, Kent State University students were protesting the Vietnam War and the Ohio National Guard on their campus. The National Guard fired into the crowd of students. Four students were killed and nine were wounded. The massacre triggered a nationwide student strike that forced hundreds of colleges and universities to close.

On January 2, 1971, because
scientific research showed that
cigarettes caused lung cancer,
a ban was made on television
advertising of cigarettes.

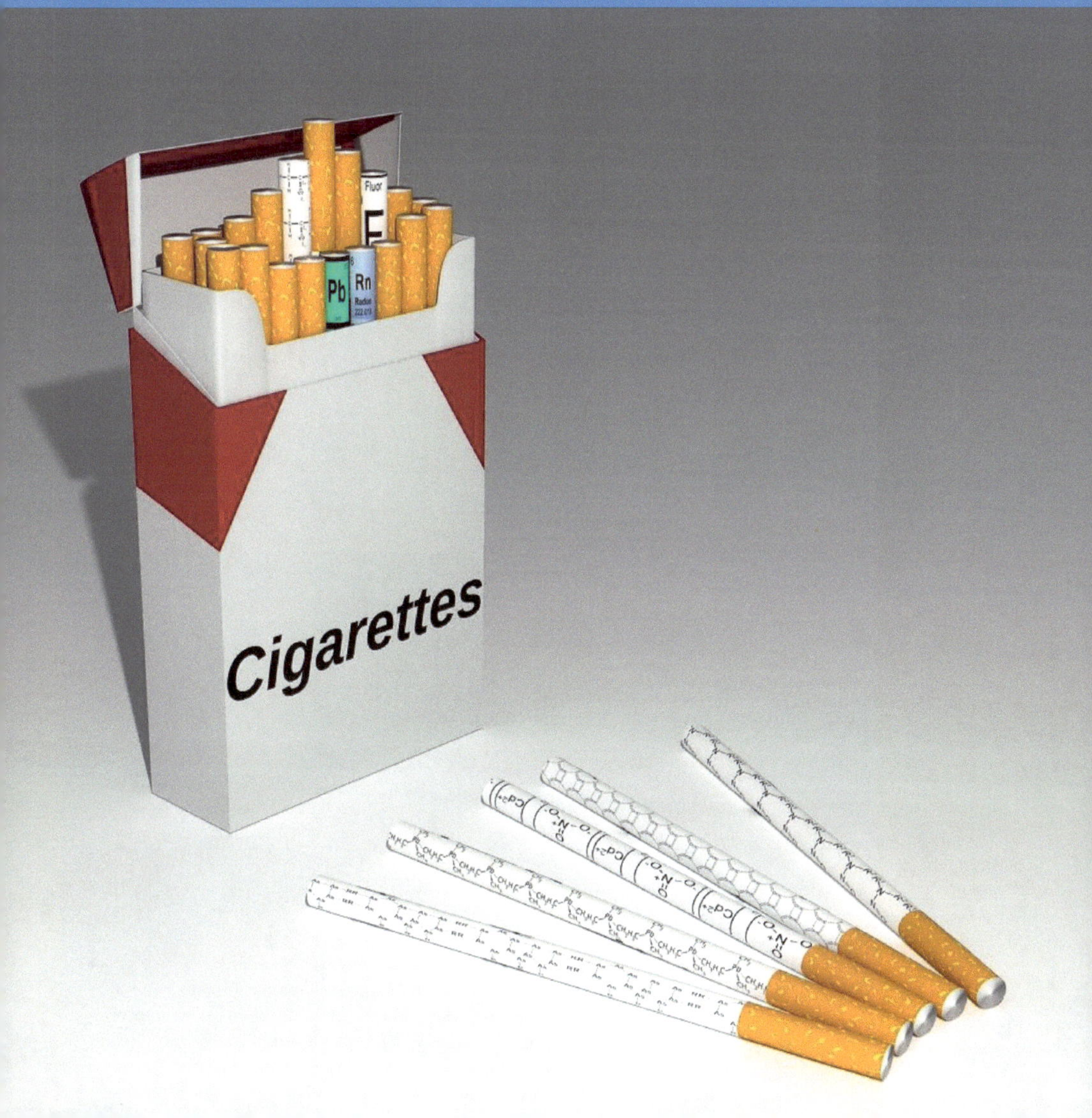

In a postal reform measure the United States Postal Service (USPS) is made independent on August 12, 1970. It was no longer supported by public subsidies. A first-class stamp that cost 5 cents in 1963 would cost 15 cents by the end of 1979.

March 1971, both the Senate and the House of Representatives approved the 26th Constitutional Amendment. Because many Americans felt that if 18 years of age was old enough to fight in a war then 18-year-olds should be able to vote. Ratified by the states on June 30th, it received certification by President Richard M. Nixon on July 5th.

On October 1, 1971, Walt Disney World opened in Orlando, Florida. Themes include Hollywood Studios, Animal Kingdom, Magic Kingdom, and Epcot Worlds of Wonder.

During the 70's, the slide rule was replaced with electronic handheld calculators like the TI-30 Texas Instrument scientific calculator that were more accurate than slide rules.

In February of 1972, President Richard M. Nixon meets with Mao Zedong. This was unprecedented at the time and began the process for normalization of relations with China.

In May of 1972, President Richard M. Nixon makes the first trip of any U.S. President to Moscow. The discussions would lead to a strategic arms agreement called SALT I (Strategic Arms Limitation Talks One) that would be signed by Nixon and Premier Leonid Brezhnev. Brezhnev visited the United States in 1973.

Designed to be a city within a city, the Watergate Complex was in the District of Columbia. It was a business and residential district. On June 17, 1972, a security guard, Frank Wills, discovered clues that former FBI and CIA agents had illegally broken into the offices of the George McGovern and the Democratic Party to get information before the Presidential election.

On November 7, 1972, Incumbent President Richard M. Nixon beat his Democratic challenger George S. McGovern. This election might be the beginning of the end for Nixon once the Watergate affair is brought to light.

December 7, 1972, Apollo 17 was the final launch of Americans to the Moon. The crew consisted of Harrison Schmitt, Eugene Cernan, and Ronald Evans. It also carried a biological experiment containing five mice named: Fe, Fi, Fo, Fum, and Phooey.

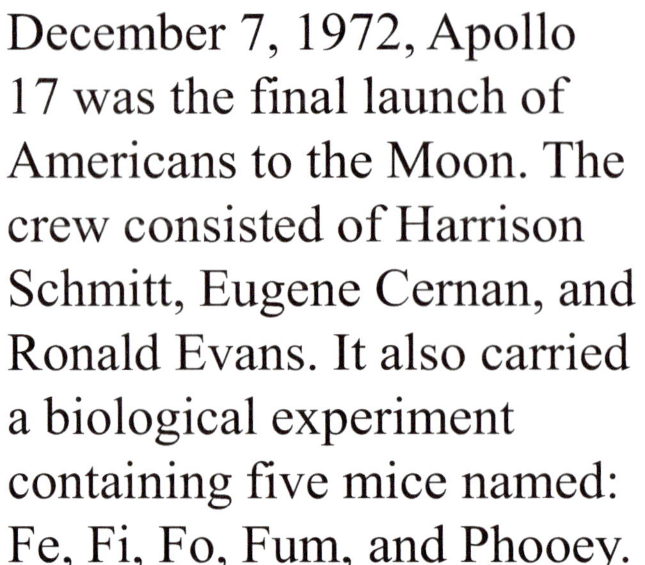

In the United States, the anti-war movement was increasing in strength. The Vietnam War was communist North Vietnam against anti-communist South Vietnam and the United States.

The Paris Peace Accords were signed in Paris, France on January 27, 1973. This agreement ended the Vietnam War. The military draft also ended on this date. The last U.S. military troops would leave the war zone on March 29, 1973.

On January 30, 1973, two defendants in the Watergate break-in trial are convicted. The remaining five defendants had pleaded guilty to the crime two weeks earlier. On April 30, 1973, Four members of the Nixon administration resign under suspicion of obstructing justice. During Senate hearings on June 25, 1973, John W. Dean would admit that the administration had conspired to cover up facts about the case.

After the start of the Arab-Israeli war, oil imports from Arab nations were banned to the United States because the U.S. supported Israel. This oil embargo created the October 1973 oil shortage that tripled oil and gasoline prices within 6 months. American cars lined up in long lines to get gasoline.

When President Nixon refused to release his recorded tapes concerning Watergate, the issue of access to the tapes went to the United States Supreme Court. On July 24, 1974, in United States versus Nixon, the Court ruled unanimously that claims of executive privilege over the tapes were not valid.

After several weeks of debate, they decided to release an edited version. Nixon announced the release of the edited transcripts in a speech to the nation on April 29, 1974. When people read the transcripts, many called for Nixon's resignation or impeachment. Nixon resigned as President on August 8, 1974.

When Nixon resigned, vice-president Gerald Ford automatically became the 38th President of the United States.

On September 8, 1974, Gerald Ford gave Nixon a full and unconditional pardon for any crimes he may have committed while President. Ford explained that he felt the pardon was in the best interests of the United States. Some people were angry that Nixon was pardoned. During the 1976 presidential election, anti-Gerald Ford buttons showed someone trying to hack into a safe labeled "Watergate".

On April 30, 1975, Communist forces complete the takeover of South Vietnam. Civilians from the United States were forced to evacuate Saigon with an unconditional surrender of South Vietnam.

On July 4, 1976, the Bicentennial
of the United States is celebrated.
The 200th anniversary paid
tribute to historical events of the
United States of America
including the American
Revolution against England and
the adoption of the Declaration of
Independence.

The Viking 1 space probe successfully lands on Mars on July 20, 1976. The first color photos of the surface of Mars are taken. The rocks and soil were eroded by wind. The iron dust blown across the surface came from ancient volcanoes.

Jimmy Carter, a former Democratic governor from Georgia, defeats Gerald Ford in the Presidential election on November 2, 1976, to become the 39th President of the United States.

Microsoft becomes a registered trademark on November 26, 1976. Microsoft was named by Bill Gates from parts of the two words "microcomputer" and "software".

Around 10,000 Vietnam War draft evaders were pardoned by President Jimmy Carter on January 21, 1977.

The movie Star Wars opens on May 25, 1977. It was the highest grossing film at that time.

Jimmy Carter created the United States Department of Energy (DOE) on August 4, 1977 . It is concerned with the United States' policies regarding energy and safety in handling nuclear material. Also, it directs research in genetics and sponsors more research in the physical sciences than any other U.S. federal agency.

On July 13, 1977, in New York City, an electrical blackout resulted in massive looting and disorderly conduct for twenty-five hours.

On September 21, 1977, the United States, the Soviet Union, and 13 other nations signed a nuclear-proliferation pact in order to stop the spread of nuclear weapons around the world, to achieve nuclear disarmament, and to promote cooperation in the peaceful uses of nuclear energy,

On April 18, 1978, the United States Senate votes to return the Panama Canal back to Panama on December 31, 1999. Completed in 1914, it was built to lower the distance, cost, and time it took for ships to carry cargo between the Atlantic and the Pacific Oceans. It cost the United States about $375 million to build the Panama Canal.

After twelve days of secret negotiations at the Camp David, Maryland retreat of the President Jimmy Carter, A Peace Agreement between Prime Minister of Israel, Menachem Begin, and President of Egypt, Anwar Sadat, was signed on September 17, 1978. Sadat and Begin were awarded the Nobel Prize for Peace.

Menachem Begin

Jimmy Carter

Anwar Sadat

An accident at the Three Mile Island nuclear power plant in Middletown, Pennsylvania occurred on March 28, 1979. There was a partial core meltdown. After five days the reactor was deemed under control. It is the largest accident in U.S. nuclear power history and considered the worst in the world until the Soviet Chernobyl nuclear power plant accident seven years later.

Anti-nuclear protests followed the Three Mile Island accident.

On September 1, 1979, the American Pioneer Eleven space probe passed the planet Saturn. It became the first spacecraft to visit the ice and dust ringed planet. It discovered conclusive evidence of the existence of Saturn's magnetic field.

Chrysler, the third largest car maker in the United States, was losing millions of dollars due to recalls of their defective Dodge Aspen and Plymouth Volare. They were on the verge of bankruptcy. The fear of millions of jobs being lost had many concerned that an already weak economy could be pushed into a depression. The federal government decided to grant a $1.5 billion loan-guarantee to assist Chrysler.

Dodge Aspen

Plymouth Volare

On November 4, 1979, the Iran Hostage Crisis began. Iranian students climbed the U.S. embassy gates in Tehran. Sixty-three Americans were among ninety hostages taken at the American embassy in Tehran. The three thousand militant student who were followers of Ayatollah Khomeini and they demanded that the former Shah Pahlavi be returned to Iran.

The Shah Pahlavi was accused of committing crimes against Iranian citizens with the help of his secret police. He had been admitted to the U.S. for cancer treatment. Iran demanded his return in order to stand trial. The hostages were held for 444 days from November 4, 1979, to January 20, 1981.

The Shah left the United States in December 1979. He was granted asylum in Egypt, where he died from cancer on July 27, 1980. Negotiations occurred in 1980 and 1981 between the United States Government and the Iranian Government to end the Iranian hostage crisis. The 52 American hostages, seized from the US Embassy in Tehran were finally released on January 20, 1981.

The Seventies saw many changes. What did we learn from the Seventies?

Some things that we learned were:

1. Race equality made advancements.

2. Peace promoted the best environment for human potential to flourish.

3. The heroism of humans.

4. Peaceful protests can have beneficial results.

5. Women's Rights advanced.

6. Science and Technology made many advances.

What else do you think that we can learn from the Seventies?

Dedicated to my lovely wife Sulastri and my grandchildren Mia and Kai as well as everyone who enjoys learning history.

For over 40 years, I have enjoyed teaching at elementary, high school and college levels.

Please follow and check out my author page at Amazon.com/author/richlinville

Illustrations from PixaBay, Wiki, and illustrations purchased from Edu-Clips.com.

Please check out my other books at bookstores and online under the name Rich Linville.

If you like learning history, you'll enjoy:

Cold War

1945 to 1991

By Rich Linville

1950 to 1959

The USA's Golden Age Begins

Ancient CHINA

2100 BC to 1912 AD

by Rich Linville

Ancient Egypt
For Kids

50,000 BC to 653 BC